BOY Talk

C. A. Plaisted
Illustrated by Chris Dickason

QEB Publishing

Illustrator: Chris Dickason
Editor: Lauren Taylor
Designer: Matthew Kelly

Consultants: John Rees and Kayla Jackson
John is a teacher, trainer, and educational consultant who works with schools, local governments, and health workers across the United Kingdom. He is committed to supporting professionals who work for young people.
    Kayla is a manager, trainer, and facilitator who works with communities, schools, and young people around the United States to ensure that they receive high-quality and accurate health information. She is dedicated to making sure that all young people are able to grow up safe and healthy in their communities.

Copyright © QEB Publishing, Inc. 2011

Published in the United States by
QEB Publishing, Inc.
3 Wrigley, Suite A
Irvine, CA 92618

www.qed-publishing.co.uk

ISBN 978 1 60992 085 2

Printed in China

Library of Congress Cataloging-in-Publication Data

Plaisted, Caroline.
  Boy talk : a survival guide to growing up / Caroline Plaisted.
     p. cm.
  Summary: "Discusses body changes that happen to boys during puberty, such as acne, body hair, body odor, mood swings, crushes, and more, and gives suggestions to teen boys for taking care of their hygiene and keeping good relationships"--Provided by publisher.
  Includes index.
  ISBN 978-1-60992-085-2 (library biniding)
  1. Boys--Juvenile literature. 2. Puberty--Juvenile literature. 3. Teenage boys--Physiology--Juvenile literature. I. Title.
  HQ775.P56 2012
  612.6'61--dc22

                                        2011009206

Website information is correct at the time of going to press. However, the publishers cannot accept responsibility for information, links, or any other content of Internet websites or third-party websites.

This book is not intended to replace the advice of professional health care. It should be used as an additional resource only. Concerns about mental or physical health should always be discussed with a doctor or professional health-care provider.

Contents

Puberty: What's It All About?

There was a time when most guys had to do tough, sweaty, dangerous jobs, which you can still do today if you choose to, but remember that men are also dancers, chefs, musicians—anything. You can be whatever you want to be, and it all starts when you grow from being a boy...

On the day you were born, you needed all the help you could get from adults to help you survive. Your brain was like a sponge, ready to soak up as much information as a super-computer! During your first year, you probably got 10 inches taller and three times heavier.

There was so much going on in your world that, by your third birthday, your brain would have been working overtime.

Now you're reaching the time of your life known as puberty—the time when your brain and body are getting ready for your exciting future.

Did You Know?

Your brain has stayed twice as active as an adult's ever since you were born! Amazing!

Q: What's the point of puberty?

A: Simple: it's to get you ready for your adult life. Puberty makes your body bigger, stronger, and fertile, which means that you'll be able to become a father, if you wish, when the time is right. It's also the time when your brain functions begin to change, allowing you to think in different ways and start being independent. By the end of puberty, you will no longer be dependent on anyone else for survival.

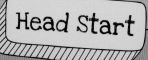

Head Start

Puberty often starts in girls before it starts in boys (irritating!), so the girls in your class may well be taller than you. But you'll catch up soon—and then you'll overtake them. Yes!

Important Point

Before you go any further, remember that puberty is different for everyone! There are no set rules, so what happens to your best friend when he is 12 years old may not happen to you until 14 or even older. There is nothing wrong if this happens—OK?

Essential Stuff

Hormones are natural chemicals produced by your brain and then pumped around your body to make everything change. This is essential stuff for puberty.

First...

A hormone leaves your brain and zooms to your pituitary gland—that's a pea-sized gland sitting at the base of your brain—where it kick-starts the production of two more hormones.

And Then...

These two hormones pump through your body to your reproductive system, where they create another hormone called testosterone. Testosterone is what's going to turn your boy's body into a man's—grrr!

Boobs for Boys

You may notice swelling or tenderness around one or both nipples at some stage. It's only temporary and may only last a few months. It's normal, and you're NOT turning into a woman. It's just your hormones going a little crazy!

The Same but Different

Boys and girls all have pretty much the same hormones as each other—they just do different things.

The Five Stages of Puberty

Remember, the ages here are all approximate, and everyone starts puberty at different times. Some boys zoom through it, and others take their time!

Stage 1 (from 9 to 12 years old). There's not much going on for anyone to see outside, but inside, your hormones are being created and are starting to make your testicles mature. At the end of Stage 1, you may find that you are suddenly getting much taller.

Stage 2 (from 9 to 15 years old). Your testicles and scrotum will gradually be getting larger, although your penis won't change much. You may begin to get some fine hair at the base of your penis. You're still getting taller and may be getting heavier.

Stage 3 (from 11 to 16 years old). You'll grow more pubic hair, and your testicles and scrotum will continue to get bigger. Although your penis is probably longer, it won't be any thicker. You'll also be growing even taller, your face may become broader, and your voice will start to deepen.

Stage 4 (from 11 to 17 years old). Your testicles and scrotum are still growing, and your penis will get longer and thicker when it's not erect. You may ejaculate sperm for the first time. Your skin will become oilier, and you'll probably get some zits. Hair will appear under your arms and on your top lip and chin.

Stage 5 (from 14 to 18 years old). You'll be nearing your full height, and your shoulders will be broader. Your genitals and pubic hair will look more like a man's, and you'll have more hair on your face and body. You may well be shaving regularly, as the hair on your face will become thicker.

With so much going on in your head during puberty, you may find that some things completely baffle you. Getting the "wiring" in your brain organized can take time, plus if you are growing fast, you can look and feel confused and clumsy. If that's the case, hang in there, things eventually work themselves out. By the end of puberty, you'll find that your brain has organized itself. It will have figured out the way you think and reason, and your decision-making skills will be complete. Other parts of your brain will be coping with your emotions and feelings.

Did You Know?

Around the age of 16 is the best time to absorb new things. It's a great time to learn stuff—especially languages and music!

Time to Snooze

Because of all that brain and body activity during puberty, you need more sleep! In fact, you need about nine and a half hours of sleep each night.

Q&A

Q: Why is everything so weird? One minute I feel OK, but the next I'm so angry I feel like exploding! What's wrong?

A: Nothing's wrong. With so much growth going on, your emotions can be all over the place. If you liked something before, you probably feel passionate about it now. If you didn't like something once, you might totally despise it these days. Instead of just feeling sad, you might feel like the world is coming to an end. Trust us—it's not. That's what it's like being a teenager. Try to relax. Soon everything will become less intense again. And remember, it's great to talk about things that are worrying you, with older brothers, your dad, uncles, grandfather, youth workers, sports coach, or teachers—anyone you feel comfortable with.

Important Point!

Your teen brain is more vulnerable than an adult one. This means the dangerous side effects of alcohol and other drugs could have much more impact and long-term consequences. It's best to stay well clear of things like that!

Skin Deep

Your skin is made up of three layers. The epidermis is the outer layer that you can see. Below that is the dermis, where the nerve endings, sweat and oil glands, and blood vessels lie. Below the dermis lie the inner layers, where hair begins to grow. It is made up mostly of fat.

blood vessel

epidermis

hair

sebaceous gland

sweat gland

Did You Know?

Your skin is actually an organ! Not only that, it is the biggest organ you have because it covers your entire body.

How Does Skin Work?

First, it's a thick layer that prevents pollution from entering your body. Every day, you shed dead skin cells when you wash or just move around. Your skin is constantly making new cells. But it uses a protein called keratin from the dead skin cells to make your skin waterproof.

Second, your skin regulates your body temperature. When it's hot, the sweat glands produce moisture to cool you down. When it's cold, the lower layer of your skin provides insulation.

Third, a layer of fat protects you against bumps and bangs and can act as a shock absorber if you fall.

Sweat It Out

Your skin is covered with little glands. If you want the fancy title, they are called sebaceous glands. There are loads of them on your forehead, nose, cheeks, and chin. Puberty hormones make these glands go berserk. Suddenly your face becomes oily, and this oil can block the pores in your skin, causing pimples. You may also notice that your skin goes from being baby smooth to feeling a little rougher as you get older.

Get the Message

There are receptors in the skin that respond to temperature, touch, and pain. They send messages and signals straight to your brain! So, next time you hurt yourself, remember to say, "Oh, good, my skin receptors are working really well"... um, if you can!

Home Stretch

Because of a rapid increase in your height and width, you might find that you get red stretch marks on the skin of your back, butt, and thighs. These will fade, becoming pale and less noticeable as you get older. Many boys don't worry about these, but if they concern you, you may find that rubbing in some special skin lotions, available from the drugstore, will make the marks less visible.

Keep It Clean

With all that oil erupting on your face, it's essential to wash your face twice every day:

★ Use a gentle cleanser made especially for teenage skin. There are many that lather up for washing your face and neck before rinsing off with a clean washcloth and lots of warm water.

★ Or you may prefer to use a cotton pad soaked in a liquid cleanser. Wipe it over your face and neck. You don't need to rinse off this kind of cleanser. And remember, always read (and follow!) the instructions.

★ Whatever type of cleanser you prefer, always make sure that you clean all of your face, including under your hair, behind your ears, and your neck.

Pimples Are the Pits!

When you get a pimple, it can make you feel really down and a little sensitive. So if you feel like teasing a boy (or girl) about their zits, remember, it could be your turn next!

Zit Zone

One of the joys of puberty (not) is pimples. They are caused by oily sebum clogging up your pores. You're not alone. At least 90% of teens get pimples at some stage in puberty. It's not a good idea to pick or squeeze pimples but, OK, everyone does—just make sure your hands and nails are clean before going anywhere near that tempting zit. You could be squeezing bacteria into an open wound—not a great move.

Blackheads can be black or yellowish. They look like bumps on your skin and may appear slightly pitted. The blocked sebum can appear black because it has reacted with the air.

Whiteheads are similar to blackheads but haven't changed color. This is because the pore isn't open and the sebum has not been exposed to the air.

Acne is an angry inflammation of the skin, usually a mixture of blackheads, whiteheads, and other types of blemishes—nice! It can be sensitive and itchy, but try to resist the urge to pick at acne. This could make it worse or even cause permanent scarring. If your acne is really bad, speak to a doctor or pharmacist.

Freckles are little brown spots on the skin caused by the sun. Everyone has pigment-producing cells in their skin called melanocytes. When the melanocytes are exposed to the sun, they make freckles on your face and body. If someone in your family has freckles or you have pale skin, you are more likely to have them. Using sun protection and keeping out of harsh sunlight will help prevent freckles.

A Hairy Situation

When puberty starts, you can feel as if you're covered in hair! It may seem annoying at times, but body hair is also important.

Hair protects your skin from germs, cushions the sensitive parts of your body, and helps you stay warm. Your body also uses the scent of your hair as a way to attract a mate, via naturally occurring chemicals called pheromones. This smell attracts others to you—dating made easy! But don't forget that there's a difference between the pheromones and unwashed socks—or armpits!

Q&A

Q: It's so embarrassing when I get changed for PE. I've got no hairs on my legs, but some other guys, well, you could almost braid their leg hairs. What's wrong with me?

A: Don't worry. Because puberty is different for everyone, hair grows at different times. And some men don't end up as hairy as others. The good news is, lots of men prefer to have a smooth body—and some girls like their guys that way, too!

Why Does Hair Grow?

Hair grows because luteinizing hormone (often called LH) is secreted by the pituitary gland. LH stimulates puberty and the start of adult hair growth.

Hairy Changes

Between the ages of 10 and 17, the hair you already have will start growing thicker, and new hair will appear. There is no "right" age for this to happen. Every boy is different. Your body hair will continue to get thicker as you grow older.

Eyebrows get thicker and darker.

Hair will start to grow on your upper lip and chin.

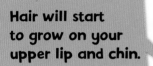

Hair will grow under your armpits.

You may get hair growing on your back and butt in your later teens.

Hair will start to grow at the base of your penis and toward your belly button as you get older.

Some boys get hairs on the back of their hands.

Your legs will grow hair. Some boys have more hair below their knees than on their thighs; other boys are equally hairy the entire length of their legs.

Shaving Rules!

★ Always use your own razor. Don't share with anyone else.

★ Never shave without covering the places you are planning to shave with a shaving foam or gel.

★ Shave downward, in the direction the hair grows, using long and even strokes.

★ Rinse your razor with water every other stroke to keep it from getting clogged with hair.

★ Shave cheeks and chin first, then upper lip. Curl your lip over your top teeth if it helps.

★ Use a styptic pencil, available from the drugstore, if you get any cuts.

★ Wash off any excess shaving foam with warm water.

★ Thoroughly clean and wash the razor before and after use.

★ Avoid using aftershave on your face. It can irritate your skin.

★ Make sure the razor blades are sharp and replaced regularly.

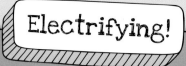
The Buzz of the Fuzz or the Shmooze of the Smooth?

Some guys prefer to have a hair-free chest and back to show off their muscles, but others think it's more "manly" to be a hairy hunk. Hairy or smooth—it's all a matter of personal preference. If you prefer to be a smoothie, shaving your chest will be time-consuming, the hair will start to grow back almost immediately, and shaving your own back is next to impossible! It's best to remove this hair by waxing, which means that hot wax is spread on your hairy parts and then ripped off with cloth strips.

Ouch!

Make no mistake, waxing off your body hair can hurt! It's also difficult to wax yourself, so it's best to get it done by a professional.

Bad Hair Days

Some older men may not understand that some boys like to use hair products or straighteners, or even different styles and hair colors—in their day it was just "short back and sides." But nowadays, boys can style their hair to make them feel or look great!

Hot Tip

Make sure you rinse your hair properly after shampooing. Soapy suds left behind make hair look dull and leave a coating that can look like dandruff.

It's a Washout

The sebaceous glands on your scalp will be working overtime during puberty, producing more sebum and making your hair greasier than before, so you may want to wash your hair every day. If you do, make sure you use a mild shampoo. Stronger shampoo has a lot of grease-fighting detergents that can be harsh on your hair and irritate your scalp.

Be Productive

If you use a lot of products, such as hair gel and styling mousse, make sure you wash them out thoroughly when you shampoo, or you'll get a buildup of gunk on your hair and scalp.

A Common Problem

Dandruff is flakes of dead skin from your scalp. Resist the urge to scratch your scalp and use a gentle dandruff shampoo. Dandruff is not contagious.

Nitwits

Most people get head lice at some times in their lives (even teachers!). If you have younger brothers and sisters, you might find that you get them, too. Lice grip your hair and are virtually invisible to the naked eye. They feed on your scalp by biting and sucking your blood like mini vampires. Then they lay their sticky white eggs (nits) in your hair. The only sure way to get rid of lice is to use a special shampoo or lotion from the drugstore and to follow the instructions carefully.

Nit-picking

It's a myth that only people with dirty hair get lice and nits! In fact, they'll leap onto anyone's scalp if they are given the chance.

Where There's a Willy, There's a Way!

Every guy has a penis. They come in a variety of shapes and sizes and get called lots of different names. Most importantly, you may be beginning to notice some changes in yours lately.

Well, What's It For?

A penis has two basic functions:

1. To let you get rid of urine.
2. For reproductive purposes—in other words, for passing sperm into a woman. Sperm are ejaculated: this is when white sticky stuff called semen shoots out from the small hole at the end of your penis.

shaft

foreskin

scrotum

Sizing It Up

Some boys worry that their penis is too small. Well, no two are the same. Penises come in all shapes and sizes; no one's is completely straight, and a larger penis is not necessarily a better penis. Size does not matter. Got it? Good!

Don't Get Hung Up

If you think your penis is too small, it almost certainly isn't, and it won't stop growing until you are 18—or maybe even as old as 21! Penises are always smaller in cold water and weather. And don't forget either that a large flaccid (soft) penis may not get much bigger when it becomes erect—and a smaller penis can nearly double in size when it's erect!

Baby Talk

Basically, when a man ejaculates during sex, semen is passed from the penis into the woman's vagina. The sperm in the semen then swim to the woman's womb (or uterus), looking for an egg to fertilize. If a sperm and an egg merge, the woman will become pregnant. However, aside from all that, there's lots of emotional stuff involved with sex that's really worth mentioning. Sex is a BIG DEAL, and should only ever happen between two people who are ready both emotionally and physically. No one should have sex because:

★ Other people boast that they are doing it.
★ A person thinks think it will make someone like them.
★ A person manages to talk someone into doing it.
★ A person thinks it will make them mature.

Contraception

A man and woman can have sex without the woman getting pregnant if they use contraception. Some methods of contraception are also used to prevent people from catching diseases (known as STIs) from each other during sex.

Most Importantly

If anyone has ever done anything physical to you that makes you feel uncomfortable or that you don't like, it's very important that you tell an adult you trust, such as a teacher.

Under Pressure

There can be a a lot of pressure on boys to boast about sex, which is dumb and disrespectful (imagine if it was your sister a boy was talking about!). Most people don't have sex until they are over 16, so there's absolutely no rush.

Erections— the Hard Facts

An erection means that you are aroused. Extra blood flows into your penis, making it grow longer and harder. You may find that during puberty, you get erections a lot, and often at embarrassing moments! It might be just because you've walked past a group of girls, or it might happen for no apparent reason at all. If you're worried that someone will notice, you could drop your bag or schoolbooks down in front of you. Some boys also find that wearing loose pants helps cover things up. And remember: most boys of your age have the same problem.

Q: There's white stuff under my foreskin. What is it, and what can I do about it?

A: It's perfectly normal, and it's called smegma. It's there to keep your foreskin lubricated. Clean behind your foreskin every day, so the smegma doesn't start to smell or make you itch.

Q: How do I keep my penis and scrotum clean?

A: With routine washing every day in the bath or shower. If you have a foreskin, gently ease it back and swish it around with water. You're better off washing your penis with just water and using a gentle soap or shower gel to clean around the rest of the genital area.

Foreskin for You

You are born with a foreskin covering the head of your penis. Sometimes, for cultural, religious, or medical reasons, the foreskin is removed. This is called circumcision. If you still have a foreskin, make sure you keep the area around the head of your penis clean to reduce the risk of infection. And remember that your penis will function completely normally whether it has a foreskin or not!

Things That Go Bump in the Night

If you notice white or yellow bumps on the skin at the head of your penis, don't pick them! They are perfectly normal. They are called papules, and they are usually nothing to worry about. But some bumps and spots can be a sign of infection—if you are worried, get them checked out by your doctor.

Ball Boy

You may find that your testicles get hard and feel uncomfortable when you have an erection. This is normal and will go away when your penis gets soft again.

Another REALLY important thing to remember is how painful and dangerous it is to get hit in the testicles or hit someone else there. So avoid it at all costs!

It's also a good idea to get used to checking your testicles in the shower or bath. They are not perfectly round and smooth, but if you notice a lump or any pain or swelling, get it checked out by a doctor as soon as possible.

Safety in Numbers

A man can produce as many as 30 million sperm every time he ejaculates.

Wet Dreams

Some boys wake up and find the sheets are wet. It's not because they've wet themselves, it's because they have ejaculated in their sleep. As you get older, wet dreams will happen less frequently and then stop altogether. Some boys have a lot of wet dreams, and some never have one at all!

Changing Shape

Puberty is a time of such rapid change that your body can seem different from one day to the next. Everyone worries about their body at some stage—that they're not tall, muscular, or hairy enough. But remember that there's no one in the whole world as good at being you as you are!

Your arms and legs may suddenly grow longer and leaner and feel like they don't belong to you. So you might become quite clumsy, tripping over or knocking things over. Your shoulders may also start to broaden before you gain weight in proportion to them, so you might feel like a skinny weakling. Don't worry! Soon your muscles will start to bulk up naturally, making your whole body look and feel much more normal!

Terrible Teasers

Some people can be really thoughtless and tease boys about changes in their body shape. Add this to all those emotional changes we've talked about and it can be upsetting. If it does all get to you, remember there are adults you can trust to talk to—folks at home, teachers, youth workers. They are all on your side and will listen.

Growing Pains

Over two or three years you may go through a massive growth spurt. It really can be possible for a shirt collar to fit one week and then be too small the next! You might want to wait until you've stopped growing before you invest in those really expensive designer jeans!

Muscle-bound

Don't get hung up on thinking you need to have a six-pack and powerful pecs. It isn't natural for teenage boys to have such finely honed muscles. In fact, it's dangerous to get into a strict weight-lifting or body-building routine when you are still growing. Just keep generally fit by exercising or taking part in sports a few times a week and your muscles will develop naturally. And remember: almost every other boy your age has many of the same concerns.

It's All in the Name

Some people think an Adam's apple looks like something stuck in your throat, like a piece of apple – hence the name Adam's apple.

Adam's Apple

Everyone has one—even girls! The correct name for it is the larynx. It's in your throat, and it's where your voice comes from. It's also known as a voice box. During puberty, a boy's larynx grows much larger than a girl's. This is because your voice is going to get stronger and deeper. At some stage, your larynx will become more noticeable and stick out a little on your neck.

Q&A

Q: My voice keeps squeaking! What's wrong?

Squeak!

A: Nothing! Your growing larynx is just geting used to its new size and sound. That's why one minute your voice seems higher and another it's deeper. It can be a pain sometimes—not knowing whether you'll growl or squeak when you open your mouth! Don't forget that half the humans on the planet will know how this feels, and it won't last forever.

Feeling Fit

No one wants to look and feel like a couch potato. But then, no one wants to exercise so much that it becomes an unhealthy obsession, either.

If you exercise and keep fit, you will:
★ Increase the "happy hormones" in your body, giving you a feel-good factor—a kind of natural high.
★ Have more energy.
★ Have fun.
★ Make new friends.
★ Have brighter skin, hair, and eyes.
★ Feel more toned and have more confidence.

If you stay a lounge lizard, you will:
★ Probably gain too much weight and have no muscle tone.
★ Have dull-looking skin, hair, and eyes.
★ Get bored.
★ Have little energy.
★ Probably have low self-esteem.
★ Miss out on fun with your friends.
★ Not meet as many new friends.

Fantastic Sports for Fit Teens

★ Team games, such as football, baseball, basketball, hockey, soccer, or rugby

★ Swimming

★ Skateboarding

★ Running

★ Cycling

★ Rowing

★ Tennis

★ Walking

★ Physically interactive computer games, such as Wii console games and dance games

★ Muscle-strengthening exercises such as squats, push-ups, and crunches

Important Point

Whatever exercise or sport you want to try, get the right clothing and protective gear to make sure you don't hurt yourself—especially your teeth and genitals!

Give It a Try!

If you're interested in a new sport, you can find out where it's happening at a local community center, gym, or on the web. New people join sports clubs all the time, so they will be happy to welcome you in.

You Are What You Eat

You start puberty with about 5 percent body fat. By the end of puberty, you will have somewhere between 8 and 20 percent, and it should stay this way throughout most of your adult life.

I'm Starving!

Because you are growing fast and burning lots of energy doing it, you're probably very hungry all the time! Make sure you eat a mixture of healthy foods and treats, and keep active. If you have lunch at school, the food available in the cafeteria is usually healthy—if you make the right choices. These good habits will keep you fit for life!

Fact no. 1

Boys can consume between 3,000 and 4,000 calories a day if they are particularly active.

Fact no. 2

Boys gain about 2 to 3 lbs every three months during puberty.

Vary It

A healthy diet is a varied one. Ideally, you should eat between three and five portions of fruits and vegetables a day. A glass of fruit juice or a smoothie can count as one portion! You also need to eat starchy, vitamin-rich foods such as bread, cereals, rice, pasta, or potatoes. If you are a meat-eater, choose meats such as chicken and fish. Cut down on salty, fatty, and sugary foods, such as chocolate, cookies, chips, butter, hot dogs, and burgers.

Wake Up and Smell the Breakfast

Don't be tempted to skip breakfast just so you can have another half hour in bed. You might be tired of hearing this, but breakfast really is the most important meal of your day. If you eat breakfast, you'll have more energy, be able to concentrate better at school, and will stay full until lunchtime. And your stomach won't rumble during morning classes—cringe! Try talking to whoever does the food shopping at home—ask for nutritious food and offer to help with the preparation and cooking—or even doing the dishes! You might enjoy it and even become a famous master chef!

Water, water Everywhere!

Don't wait until you feel thirsty to take a drink, because by that time, your body is already beginning to dehydrate! Try to drink water instead of sugary soft drinks. Water is better for your teeth, more refreshing, costs nothing if you drink tap water, and is calorie-free!

Weight Worries

It's not only girls who worry about their weight. Boys can get hung up about dieting, too. Food is an essential part of living, and one of the best things about it is enjoying eating it. If you eat too much and don't exercise, or eat too little and exercise obsessively, you can get really sick. Anorexia nervosa and bulimia are two eating disorders that can develop during the teenage years. Sufferers can get tired easily, lose teeth and the hair on their head, and have low self-esteem. If you are worried that you or someone you know may have an eating disorder, it's very important to speak to an adult about your concerns.

Your sight and your eyes are precious, so you need to take care of them. Make sure you:

★ Get regular exercise: eyes need oxygen to stay healthy, and staying active will increase the oxygen supply to your body.

★ Don't spend too much time in front of the TV or computer screen. The glare can strain your eyes.

★ Get enough sleep to rest your eyes.

★ See your eye doctor regularly: even if you don't think you have a problem, have a check-up. The doctor can see inside your eyes, too, and make sure everything is OK.

★ If you have glasses, wear them when you're supposed to: not doing so will make your eyes tired and sore.

★ Protect your eyes from the sun: wear sunglasses in the summer and goggles if you go skiing.

Glasses: The Long and Short of It

If you are short-sighted, it means that you find it difficult to see things at a distance—like movie screens or street signs. If you are long-sighted, it means you struggle to read books or text on screens. The great news is that, if you have to wear glasses, you will have loads of styles to choose from, and some girls might really fancy you (think of how intelligent you'll look!). If you do a lot of sport, select a pair of flexible frames and maybe get a band that attaches to your glasses and secures them to your head. You can also get prescription goggles if you do a lot of swimming.

Handle with Care

To keep your specs in top-notch condition:

★ Keep them clean using the cloth in your case or use a special lens cleaner.
★ Don't put your glasses down and leave them resting on the lenses as they will get scratched.
★ Keep your glasses in their case when you aren't wearing them.

Make Contact

Even though glasses are extremely cool, if you're fed up with them, you could consider contact lenses. You will need to ask your optician to see if contacts are right for you. They need to be kept in a special solution when not being worn, or they can damage your eyes. Many people wear disposable contact lenses, which are much easier to care for.

Champion Chompers

You need your teeth to eat and to communicate, so you don't want them to be decayed or dirty. Keeping your teeth clean now will set you up for life!

Remember to:

★ Brush your teeth twice a day for about two minutes each time.

★ Brush in small circles, not across or up or down.

★ Use a fluoride toothpaste and a toothbrush that's right for your age.

★ Clean between your teeth with floss once a day, preferably before bedtime.

★ Change your toothbrush regularly. You'll know it needs to be changed when the bristles start to curl at the top.

The Last Straw

It's best to sip soda and fruit juice through a straw, so less sugar gets on your teeth. Also, don't brush your teeth right after drinking sugary drinks, because it can soften the enamel. It's better to wait about 30 minutes and rinse your mouth with water before brushing.

Mega Molars

You'll have most of your adult teeth by the time you are 14 years old, but there will be some molars that wait until you're 17 or even older before erupting. These are your third molars and are most commonly known as wisdom teeth. Lots of people don't have enough space in their mouth for wisdom teeth, so dentists like to check them regularly.

Close Contact!

If you play any kind of contact sport (such as hockey, basketball, or football), always wear protection for your teeth. A mouthguard can prevent broken teeth and damage to your gums. You can buy one at most sporting-goods stores. Follow the instructions to make the mouthguard fit your own mouth.

Brace Yourself

Lots of teens wear braces because their teeth are crooked, overcrowded, or don't bite together properly. Braces may have to be worn for a few months or up to three years. If you wear braces, always make sure you follow your orthodontist's advice about keeping your teeth and braces clean —there's no point having lovely, straight teeth just to let them decay, is there? No one is crazy about having a mouth full of metal, but it will be worth it in the end. Just think of that smile and the trips to the dentist you'll avoid when you are older!

What a Stinker!

Bad breath can be caused by smoking, certain foods, not brushing your teeth properly, and, rarely, because of a medical disorder. Brushing your teeth, gums, and tongue regularly will usually keep smelly breath at bay. If it doesn't, speak to your dentist.

Clean Up Your Act!

All day, every day, your skin is producing sebum and sweat and, at the same time, shedding dead skin cells. Bacteria, found in the air around us, join this mixture whether you like it or not and—ta-da!—your body starts to smell. Actually, in some boys some parts of their body start to smell stronger than others. This smell is known as body odor (BO for short).

You can keep the smell under control by:

★ Washing every day, preferably in the shower or bath.
★ Drying thoroughly everywhere after washing.
★ Hanging your towel up after you have used it, and changing it every few days.
★ Using an antiperspirant deodorant to stop your armpits from smelling.
★ Wearing a clean shirt every day.
★ If you wear a school uniform, changing out of it when you get home. Hang the uniform up to air when you aren't wearing it.
★ Always showering after exercise and changing into fresh clothes afterward.

Sniff It Out!

If you suspect that you have a little BO, don't wait for someone to tell you that you stink before you do something about it. Get into a routine of washing regularly, and you won't have to worry about it.

Deodor-Don't

Lots of boys like to wear deodorant to make sure they smell good. But be warned: deodorant won't cover up the stink of sweat underneath. You need to wash before you spray it on. Also, make sure you wash regularly to rinse away the smell you sprayed on earlier. If you don't, the body spray itself will start to smell stale and it will also block pores, adding to the likelihood of BO.

Feet First

Feet are often the first things to grow when puberty kicks in. They may increase in size so rapidly that you'll outgrow new shoes in no time! Some boys find that their feet have reached their full size by the time they're 15.

Q&A

Q: My feet really stink—even I can smell them! How can I stop them from reeking?

A: There are a number of things you can do:

★ Wash your feet every day and dry them thoroughly.
★ Wear clean cotton socks daily.
★ Wear different socks for sports, and change out of them afterward.
★ Don't wear sneakers all the time. Alternate with leather or other well-ventilated shoes.
★ When you take your shoes off, leave them someplace where they can air.
★ Keep toenails clean and short.
★ Go barefoot at home for at least some of the time.
★ Use deodorizing insoles and foot powder, available from the drugstore.

The Big Stink

Your feet are covered in sweat glands that contain salt and water, which are secreted out constantly. Imagine cramming those feet inside a pair of shoes for a day and mixing all that sweat with bacteria in your shoes and socks—it's a steamy thought, isn't it? And it's also a smelly one. Having smelly feet is technically called bromohydrosis. But it doesn't really matter what it's called, because it still honks.

Wicked Warts

Everyone's heard of warts, but few people will admit to having one. That's a pity, because warts are highly contagious. Officially, the warts on the soles of your feet are known as plantar warts. They have been pushed to the surface of the skin on the sole of your foot by the weight of your body.

Locker Rooms!

All that walking around barefoot in the locker rooms at school and the local swimming pool makes you vulnerable to plantar warts. To avoid the infections that cause them, you should try...

★ Not walking around barefoot while you change.
★ Standing on a towel when your socks are off.
★ Walking to the poolside in flip-flops or watersport shoes.
★ Wearing special swim socks—these are available from sporting-goods stores, drugstores, and some swimming pools. You should also wear these if you have a wart to stop anyone else from catching it!

Your Family and Other Animals

Pesky Parents

Let's admit it: sometimes you take your parents (or whoever cares for you at home) for granted. They do pretty much everything for you. But they take something for granted, too: that they're in charge. Sometimes it can feel like your folks are trying to rule your life. The thing is, when they were your age, they used to feel the same way. So talk to older people you can trust, not just about problems and worries, but about all the terrific things in your life. They may not understand just how hard that computer game level really is, but they care about you and want the best for you. They might even let you have an extra 10 minutes on that noisy drum kit or guitar game if they know how much it means to you!

Stupid Siblings

Your older brothers and sisters probably seem to spend all their time pushing you around. And the younger ones? They drive you nuts being in your face all day and wanting you to play their baby games.

And Then There's You...

You are getting older and you want to be treated like an adult. But on the other hand, sometimes you just can't cope with the responsibility people expect of you. You've got pressure at school. You want to spend time with your friends. And sometimes, you just want to sit at home and play video games or be spoiled rotten by your grandma! One minute you are happy, the next minute you feel like stomping around in anger—and you don't even know why!

Let's take a minute to chill out. There are ways to cope with your family relationships. Try to remember:

★ There's no rush to grow up.
★ Don't keep your friends a secret from your parents—bring them back to the house to hang out.
★ If you want to be treated like an adult, don't throw toddler tantrums.
★ Your parents love you a whole lot; they are not your enemies.
★ Talk to your parents about how you feel, and listen to their point of view.
★ Ask if you can have more privacy. If you share a bedroom, try to work out a way for you and your sibling to each have personal space.
★ Spend a little time with your family. If you never do, then you'll never be able to have any fun with them.

Totally Crushed

There's a girl at school that you can't stop thinking about, but you are too shy to speak to her. Or maybe there's a dead cool PE teacher. You wish you were like him and dressed like him...

Welcome to the world of crushes. It's like having a minor obsession with someone—anyone! It could be a girl, a boy, a teacher, a celebrity—whoever it is, it's perfectly normal. When you have a crush, the intense feelings might feel like they're taking over your life, but eventually they will die down.

Q&A

Q: Lately I've started to have feelings for another boy. Aren't I supposed to only like girls?

A: Loads of kids have same-sex crushes during puberty—they just might not admit it! Everyone has their own preferences for crushes—some boys like girls with dark hair, some boys like girls with light hair, and some boys like boys! If, when you are older, you still like people of your own sex, that's absolutely fine.

The ... about ...

You might ... be a real ... they might ... like you and ... completely ... Just remember ... age are also g... puberty, so th... can be all ... place, ...

Best Buds

When you start junior high or middle school, you'll meet a whole bunch of new friends. But try not to drop your old ones. As you get older, your friendship circle will be made up of lots of different people.

The key to having great friends is recognizing the ones who are good for you and those who aren't. Talk to someone you trust if you feel unhappy about any of your friendships.

FRIENDSHIPS SHOULD:
★ be fun.
★ make you feel good.
★ be reliable.

FRIENDSHIPS SHOULDN'T:
★ make you feel bad about yourself.
★ make you feel insecure.
★ be hard work.
★ tempt you into things that you feel unhappy about.

The Trouble with Drugs

As you grow up to become a teenager, you'll have all sorts of awesome things to look forward to, but there are also some things to avoid or be careful of. Other guys might encourage you to smoke cigarettes or take other drugs—how stupid is that? Drugs affect young, growing people even more than they do adults, and can lead to some really nasty consequences.

A Drinking Problem

The problem with alcohol (besides being illegal before the age of 21) is that it can make people do crazy things. And sure, crazy things can be funny sometimes, but not when they lead you to do something dangerous or violent. Alcohol in moderation might be OK for some adults, but this is a decision to make when you're older.

Remember that they are your decisions; doing something just because you think other people are doing it, or letting other people decide what happens to you, is just plain crazy!

Cool School

Some say that school days are the best of your life, but you might not agree with that right now. Even if you don't like all your subjects, and some of your teachers seem a little weird, the fact is that you have to spend a lot of time at school, so you might as well do your best to enjoy it.

Q&A

Q: We have to take so many stupid subjects. I can't see the point —why should I bother?

A: The way you feel is understandable, but you need to take these subjects so you can get into high school, and maybe college. Without at least a high school diploma, it will be really tough to get a job. When you're about to throw in the pencil, try to focus on the goal at the end, and think positive thoughts: "If I just push through and get decent grades, I am paving the way for a better future!"

Q: I'm starting at a new school soon. How can I make sure I fit in?

A: Everyone is a little nervous when starting at a new school. Just be yourself and make it clear that you want to make friends. Don't try to big yourself up, thinking it will impress people. You're bound to trip yourself up with your fibs and end up losing friends. You don't have to change the way you dress or behave to get attention or to blend in with others. You'll soon find friends who like you for who you are.

Bullying Boys

There's always someone who wants to be the loudest, funniest, most attention-grabbing person at school. And that's fine, as long as they don't go about it by making fun of someone else. Bullies don't just use their size or strength to scare people. They do it by excluding people, too—maybe by spreading rumors online or by gossiping, or by speaking to people in a way that makes them feel humiliated. Bullies don't just do it on their own: most of them have a gang behind them. The truth is, their leader is really a coward who is too scared to do the bullying on his or her own, and the gang is too scared to stand up to the leader.

It's Not Just Boys...

Girls can be bullies, too! Not just with other girls, either. If a girl is giving you a hard time, don't be embarrassed about telling your teacher.

Stand Proud!

You can stand up to bullies by not letting them get away with it. Your school should have a policy about bullying—speak to the person who is in charge of it or to a teacher you trust. And if you see someone else being bullied (even if it's someone you don't know or like,) stand up for them. No one ever has to know that you told someone about it, and you might be saving someone a whole lot of trouble!

Networking

I t's great talking to friends on your computer or cell, but your parents just don't get it. When they were your age, they didn't have cell phones or social networking sites, so no wonder they don't understand why you're having so much fun.

Hanging on the Telephone

Your phone is your lifeline to independence. Don't risk losing it!

Don't:
★ Rack up a big bill.
★ Ignore your parents when they try to contact you.
★ Use your phone during school unless you have permission to.
★ Leave your phone in a stupid place or make it easy for someone to steal it.
★ Send crude texts or photos to anyone (even if it seems funny at the time).
★ Forward any viral messages you receive.
★ Plug earphones into your ears when you're on a busy street, or anyplace where you need your hearing.

Do:
★ Use your phone to keep in touch with your parents.
★ Keep it switched on when you are with your friends.
★ Keep it charged at all times.
★ Tell an adult if you are being hassled via your phone.
★ Delete any viral messages that other kids are spreading.
★ Only give your number to people you know and trust.
★ Keep aware when using your phone outside.
★ Take your phone out of your pocket before your clothes are washed!

Use Your Cyber Sense

The Internet is a great way to keep in touch, but it can be a tricky place to stay safe in. And the things you intend to say privately are really not private at all. Pay attention to these wise words:

★ Keep your password secret and change it every so often.

★ Keep your friendship groups to only the people you know 100 percent—don't include people you've never met, no matter how friendly they seem.

★ Only put up posts, photos, and comments that won't embarrass or humiliate you or your friends (or even people you don't especially like).

★ Lock your profile so others can't meddle with it, and don't mess with other people's profiles.

★ Remember that teachers, colleges, and even future employers may check social networking sites to see what you've been up to. What seemed funny last night might not seem so clever tomorrow.

★ Remember that even if you delete something you regret posting earlier, someone may already have saved it elsewhere. What you put on the Internet is there forever.

★ Don't let someone coax you into doing or saying something online that you feel uncomfortable about. Report cyber pests and bullies to site monitors.

Glossary

adolescence / adolescent The time in your life also known as puberty / someone who is going through puberty.

anorexia nervosa An eating disorder characterized by the fear of becoming overweight, resulting in excessive dieting and exercising, illness, and even death.

anus The hole in your bottom where solid waste comes out when you go to the bathroom.

bulimia nervosa An eating disorder characterized by eating large amounts of food in short bursts, and then vomiting afterward. It can result in illness, and even death.

cervix The entrance to the womb at the top of the vagina.

contraception The general name for different ways to stop a woman from becoming pregnant.

dandruff Flakes of dead skin from your scalp.

ejaculate/ejaculation The ejection or discharge of sperm from the penis.

follicle A tiny hole in your skin where a hair grows. You have many follicles.

gland A cell or organ that makes chemical substances and then releases them for the body to use or get rid of.

hormone A chemical substance made by a gland and then carried around the body.

keratin A protein found in the outer layer of skin which makes it waterproof; keratin is also found in nails and hair.

perspiration A salty fluid released by the sweat glands of the skin; it is also called sweat.

pheromone A chemical substance produced by humans and other animals. We are not aware of our own, but they can affect the responses of others.

pituitary gland A gland attached to a stalk at the base of the brain, which releases hormones relating to skeletal growth and the reproductive system.

puberty The time in your life, also known as adolescence, when your body prepares itself for adulthood.

pubic hair Hair on the genital area.

scrotum The pouch of skin containing the testes, or testicles.

sebum The oily substance that acts as a lubricant for the hair and skin.

semen The thick, whitish liquid containing sperm that is ejaculated from the penis.

smegma A whitish *sebaceous* substance that lubricates the foreskin.

sperm Male reproductive cells; also known as spermatozoa.

sweat A salty fluid released by the sweat glands of the skin.

testicles The two reproductive glands that produce sperm.

testosterone A hormone secreted by the testes.

uterus An organ, lying within a woman's abdomen, in which a baby grows before it is born. Also called the womb.

vagina The tube that leads from the cervix of the womb to an outer opening, between the urethra and anus.

Index

Notes for Parents and Teachers

We talk to girls about puberty, especially periods, but we don't seem to talk to boys as much. These can be turbulent times for young people and their families and teachers, and research has shown the importance of establishing and maintaining relationships with boys from childhood into adulthood. It can feel daunting, but this book is designed to help boys (although their sisters might also find it interesting) through this transformation.

- Familiarize yourself with this book and learn when and how to describe the physical changes, adult emotions, or themes in a way that a child can understand.

- Many boys find it hard to discuss their feelings, so you may prefer to let him read this book on his own, and then invite questions later.

- Don't try to give all the information at once. Offer small amounts and invite him to question you.

- Try talking in informal situations, such as on a walk, playing catch, or even watching TV.

- Taking an interest in his hobbies and praising him (rather than the nagging that some youngsters complain about) can make a big difference.

- Boys need positive male role models in their lives. Older cousins, uncles, youth workers, and grandfathers are all potential role models—and boys often need to talk with someone outside their immediate family.

- Teachers are incredibly important. Check that your school policy supports you teaching and answering questions. If it doesn't, find out what you can do to update it.

The boys in our care will mirror the ways that we treat them and treat each other. The personal relationships we build with them can prepare them to deal with any difficult times they may face. They need and deserve a solid foundation of love and trust, based on honest, open communication.